all CREATURES
Stitched and Small

What charming creatures! Lori Markovic's La-D-Da Designs are always a delight to see, and these sweet beasts are no exception. Why not stitch a stretching cat, a band of woodland friends, or a fun silhouette of Noah's Ark? Let a tiger leap through the forest while an elephant trumpets nearby. And of course, the dogs will want to go for a run—just for fun! Lori's little animals are so easy to capture in cross stitch, you may end up stitching the whole whimsical menagerie!

Meet Lori Markovic

If you're just discovering the design work of Lori Markovic, you're in for a real treat! In each of her La-D-Da cross stitch pieces, Lori combines the homey appeal of primitive samplers with a touch of modern flair.

"I started cross-stitching when my children were little," says Lori. "Then, a little over a decade ago, some vintage sampler books caught my eye at the library. I wanted to try designing a sampler, because I was thinking a lot about the girls who stitched those Early American pieces. Their lives were all about family, home, and faith—ideals that run through all generations. And that's how I started La-D-Da Designs."

Lori and husband Bob live in Wisconsin, where they are happily surrounded by family. Lori likes to garden and bird watch, which no doubt inspires many of the natural elements in her designs. Another inspiration is the strong sense of community she enjoys with fellow cross-stitchers.

Lori says, "As a designer, I've had the opportunity to meet many stitchers across this country and am amazed by their generosity and kindness. Cross stitch is truly a gentle art for gentle souls."

LEISURE ARTS, INC.
Little Rock, Arkansas

All of the animals except for man know that the principle business of life is to enjoy it.
—Samuel Butler

Chart is on pages 8 and 9.

*J*n all things of nature
there is something of the
marvelous.

—Aristotle

Chart is on pages 10 and 11.

The reason a dog has so many friends is that he wags his tail instead of his tongue.
—Author Unknown

Chart is on pages 12 and 13.

The Elephant

When people call this beast to mind,
They marvel more and more
At such a little tail behind,
So large a trunk before.

—Hilaire Belloc   Chart is on pages 14 and 15.

God made the cat so that man might have the pleasure of caressing the tiger.
—Fernand Méry

Chart is on pages 16 and 17.

Of clean beasts, and of beasts that are not clean, and of fowls, and of every thing that creepeth upon the earth, there went in two and two unto Noah into the ark, the male and the female, as God had commanded Noah.

Genesis 7:8-9, KJV

Chart is on pages 18 and 19

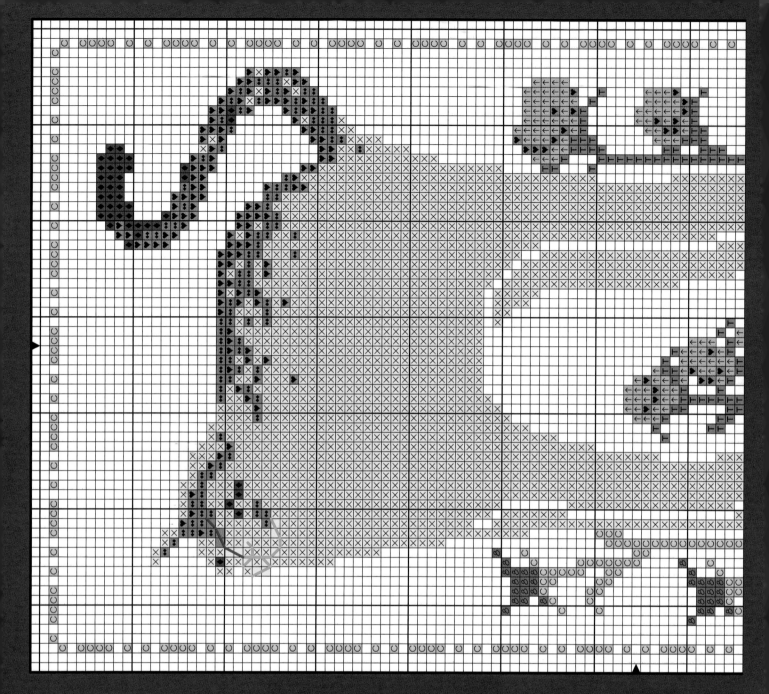

White Cat

(shown on page 2) was
stitched over 2 fabric threads
on a 10" x 13½" piece of
Sheep's Straw Linen by R&R
Reproductions (35 count).
One strand of Weeks Dye
Works floss was used for
Cross Stitch and 2 strands
for Backstitch. Personalize
the design by adding the
stitcher's initials and the year
stitched using the alphabet
and numbers on page 20. The
design size is 3¾" x 7⅜". The
design was custom framed.
Before beginning, familiarize
yourself with the **General
Instructions**, pages 21-23.

Stitch Count: (64w x 127h)

14 count	4⅝" x 9⅛"
16 count	4" x 8"
18 count	3⅝" x 7⅛"

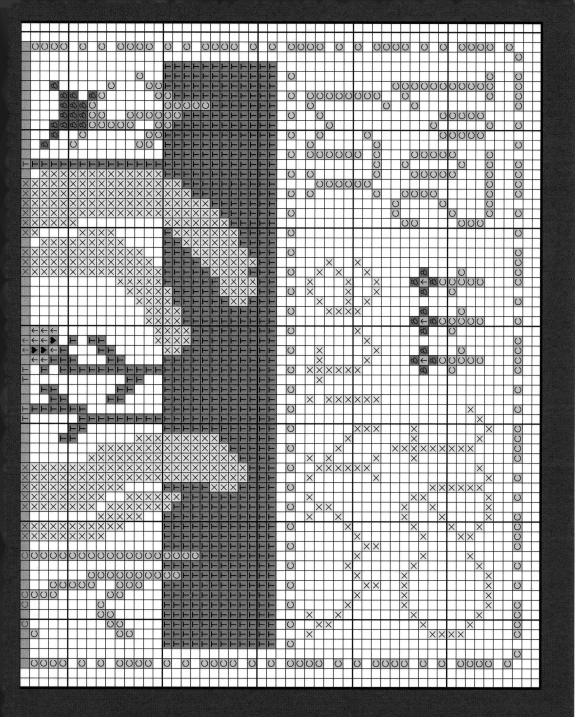

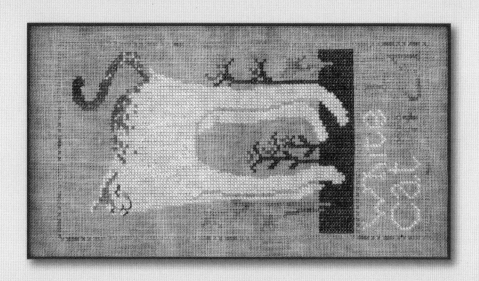

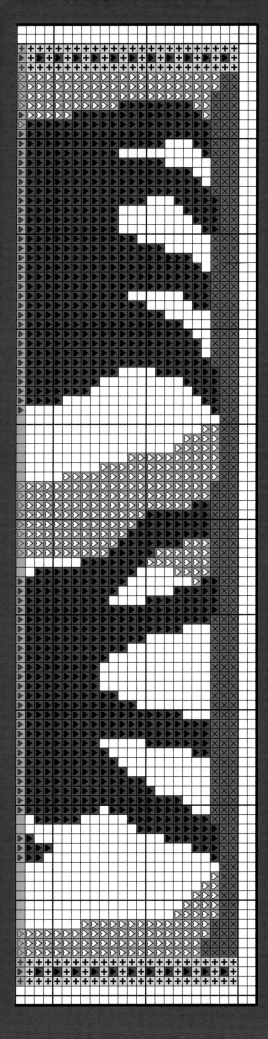

Trek in the Woods

(shown on page 3) was stitched over 2 fabric threads on an 11" x 11" piece of Blue Mood Java by R&R Reproductions (40 count). One strand of Sampler Threads from The Gentle Art was used for Cross Stitch. Design size is 5" x 5". The design was custom framed. Before beginning, familiarize yourself with the **General Instructions**, pages 21-23.

				Stitch Count:	(99w x 99h)
				14 count	7¹/₈" x 7¹/₈"
				16 count	6¹/₄" x 6¹/₄"
				18 count	5¹/₂" x 5¹/₂"

X	SAMPLER THREADS	DMC	SUL	COLOR	
	Nutmeg	435	45096	gold	
	Shaker White	543	45122	beige	
	Forest Glade	935	45277	green	
	Dark Chocolate	3371	45351	brown	
	Mulberry	3777	45390	red	
	Indicates last row of top section.				

Three Dogs-a-Leaping

(shown on page 4) was stitched over 2 fabric threads on a 14" x 11½" piece of Norfolk Blend Linen by R&R Reproductions (32 count). One strand of Needlepoint, Inc. Silk floss was used for Cross Stitch and Backstitch. Personalize the design by adding the stitcher's initials and the year stitched using the alphabet and numbers on page 20. For small pink flowers in grass, refer to **Wrapped Flowers**, page 23. Design size is 7¾" x 5½". The design was custom framed. Before beginning, familiarize yourself with the **General Instructions**, pages 21-23.

X	NPI	B'ST	DMC	SUL	COLOR
H	991bb		blanc	45001	white
8	222		223	45045	pink
～	863		301	45049	terra-cotta
■	993		310	45053	black
X	643		520	45117	green
♥	315		610	45143	brown
C	973		640	45148	taupe
◆◆	345		730	45174	olive
T	333		731	45175	lt olive
❮	312		833	45234	green gold
▲	348	╱	935	45277	dk green
◆	967		3021	45428	dk brown
♥	533		3328	45339	salmon
■	Indicates last row of left section.				

Stitch Count: (123w x 87h)

14 count	8⅞" x 6¼"
16 count	7¾" x 5½"
18 count	6⅞" x 4⅞"

Sachi the Elephant

(shown on page 5) was stitched over 2 fabric threads on a 13½" x 12" piece of Sheep's Straw Linen by R&R Reproductions (35 count). Two strands of Needlepoint, Inc. Silk floss were used for beige Cross Stitch. One strand was used for remaining Cross Stitch and Backstitch. Personalize the design by adding the stitcher's initials and the year stitched using the alphabet and numbers on page 20. Design size is 7¼" x 5⅝". The design was custom framed. Before beginning, familiarize yourself with the **General Instructions**, pages 21-23.

X	NPI	B'ST	SAMPLER THREADS	DMC	SUL	COLOR
e	863		Burnt Orange	301	45049	terra-cotta
■	993	◪	Black Crow	310	45053	black
✚	952		Cidermill Brown	610	45143	brown
♥	972		Banker's Grey	640	45148	dk beige
✕	335		Tarnished Gold	830	45231	olive gold
◆	348		Forest Glade	936	45278	dk green
✳	642		Evergreen	3363	45349	green
▼	605		Hyacinth	3740	45371	violet
♡	984		Straw Bonnet	3782	45394	beige
T	127		Claret	3802	45399	mauve

■ Indicates last row of left section.

Stitch Count: (126w x 97h)

14 count	9" x 7"
16 count	7⅞" x 6⅛"
18 count	7" x 5½"

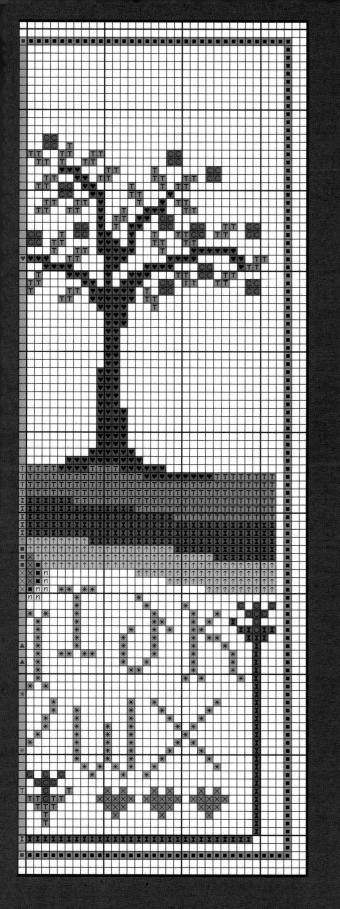

Leaping Cat

(shown on page 6) was stitched over 2 fabric threads on a 13" x 12" piece of hand-dyed linen (36 count). One strand of Sampler Threads from The Gentle Art was used for Cross Stitch and Backstitch. Personalize the design by working the stitcher's initials in brown floss and adding the year stitched using the numbers on page 20. Design size is 6⅞" x 5¾". The design was custom framed. Before beginning, familiarize yourself with the **General Instructions**, pages 21-23.

X	SAMPLER THREADS	B'ST	DMC	SUL	COLOR
■	Black Crow	□*	310	45053	black
n	Summer Meadow		676	45156	gold
✳	Grecian Gold		831	45232	dk gold
C	Mulberry		918	45264	copper
▲	Old Blue Paint		932	45275	blue
⊠	Forest Glade		936	45278	dk green
✕	Nutmeg		975	45304	rust
↑	Avocado		3012	45317	lt green
T	Shutter Green		3363	45349	green
♥	Maple Syrup		3781	45393	brown
▨	Indicates last row of left section.				

* Use long stitches for whiskers.

Stitch Count: (123w x 102h)

14 count	8⅞" x 7⅜"
16 count	7¾" x 6⅜"
18 count	6⅞" x 5¾"

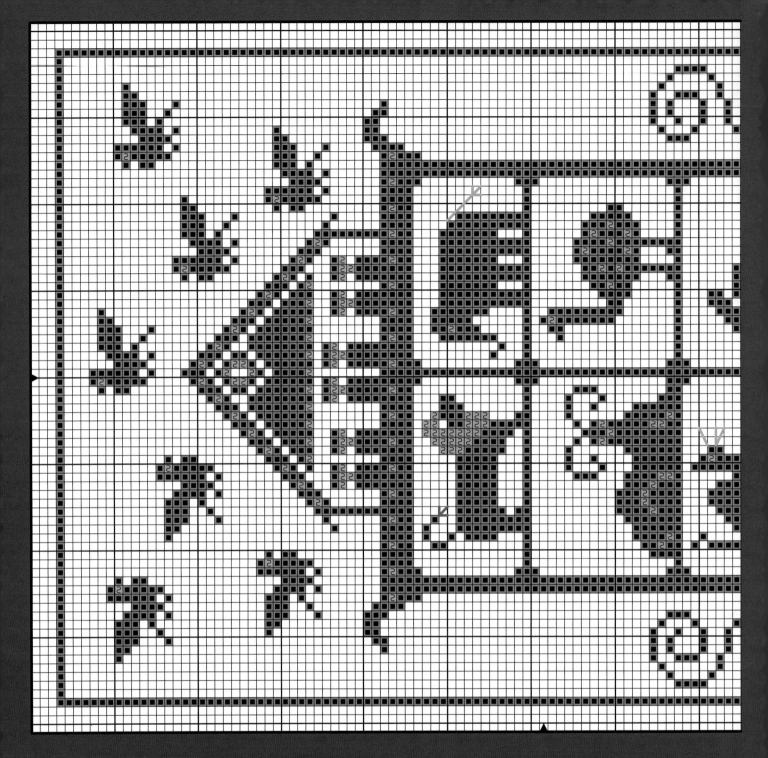

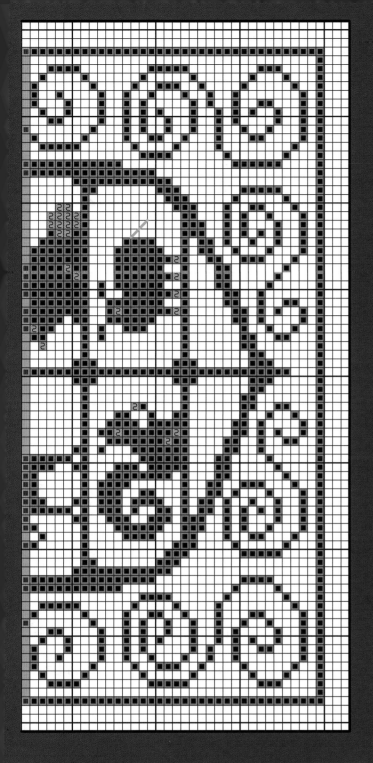

X	NPI	B'ST	DMC	SUL	COLOR
■	993	╱	310	45053	black
◨	952	╱	611	45144	tan
▨				Indicates last row of top section.	

Stitch Count: (76w x 117h)

14 count	5½" x 8⅜"
16 count	4¾" x 7⅜"
18 count	4¼" x 6½"

The Ark

(shown on page 7) was stitched over 2 fabric threads on a 10½" x 12½" piece of hand-dyed linen (36 count). One strand of Needlepoint, Inc. Silk floss was used for Cross Stitch and Backstitch. Design size is 4¼" x 6½". The design was custom framed. Before beginning, familiarize yourself with the **General Instructions**, pages 21-23.

Alphabet

Designer Tip:
Lori altered her initials
and dates, "nesting"
and offsetting the
letters and numbers for
a unique design. Use
this alphabet as is, or
change it as you like.

General Instructions

Using Hand-dyed Flosses and Fabrics

Hand-dyed flosses and linens have variations, sometimes very subtle, in shading. In order to maintain these variations, it is safer to not wash your hand-dyed items, before or after stitching. Wash your hands before each stitching session and keep your project in a clean location while not stitching.

Determining the Size to Cut Your Fabric

1. The stitch count, width and height, is provided for each project. The design size is also listed for certain fabric thread counts. To determine the design size for fabric thread counts not listed, follow Steps 2 and 3.
2. Divide the width number by the thread count of your fabric. This gives you the width of your design in inches when stitched on that particular count fabric.

Examples

63 squares wide ÷ 14 count Aida = 4$\frac{1}{2}$" wide
63 squares wide ÷ 18 count Aida = 3$\frac{1}{2}$" wide
63 squares wide ÷ 28 count linen over 2 threads
    = 4$\frac{1}{2}$" wide

3. Repeat the process to determine the height of the design.
4. When cutting the fabric, add at least 3" to each side of the design.

Working with Floss

If using more than one strand of floss, separate strands and realign them before threading your needle to ensure smoother stitches. Keep stitching tension consistent. Begin and end floss by running it under several stitches on the back; never tie knots.

How to Read Charts

Each chart is made up of a key and a gridded design where each square represents a stitch. The symbols in the key tell which floss color to use for each stitch in the chart. The floss type used in the photo model is listed in the key first, then other flosses which may be used instead arc listed with their conversion numbers or names. Use the same number of strands indicated regardless of the type of floss you choose. Be aware that using a different floss will give your stitched piece a different appearance. The following headings and symbols may be included:

X – Cross Stitch
B'ST – Backstitch
DMC – DMC floss color number
SUL – Sullivans floss color number
SAMPLER THREADS – Sampler Threads or Simply Shaker Sampler Threads from The Gentle Art color name
WEEKS – Weeks Dye Works floss color name
NPI – Needlepoint, Inc. Silk floss color number
COLOR – The name given to the floss color in this chart

A square filled with a color and a symbol should be worked as a Cross Stitch.

A straight line should be worked as a Backstitch unless noted otherwise.

In the chart, the symbol for a Cross Stitch may be omitted or partially covered when a Backstitch crosses its square. Refer to the background color to determine the floss color.

How to Stitch

Always work Cross Stitches first and then add the Backstitch.

Cross Stitch (**X**): If using hand-dyed floss (The Gentle Art Sampler Threads or Weeks Dye Works floss), work one complete Cross Stitch at a time before moving to the next Cross Stitch (**Fig. 1**). This applies to working horizontally or vertically. When working over 2 fabric threads, work Cross Stitch as shown in **Fig 2**.

If using DMC, Sullivans, or silk floss, work as follows: For horizontal rows, work stitches in two journeys (**Fig. 3**). For vertical rows, complete each stitch as shown (**Fig. 4**). When working over 2 fabric threads, work Cross Stitch as shown in **Fig. 5**.

Fig. 1

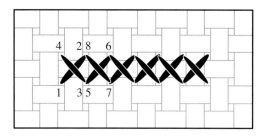

Fig. 2

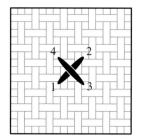

Fig. 3

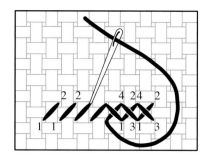

Fig. 4

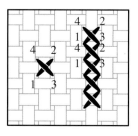

Fig. 5

Backstitch (B'ST): For outlines and details, Backstitch should be worked after all Cross Stitches have been completed (**Fig. 6**). When working over 2 fabric threads, work Backstitch as shown in **Fig 7**.

Fig. 6

Fig. 7

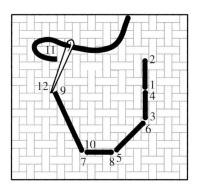

Wrapped Flowers: After all Cross Stitches and Backstitches are completed, use 1 strand of pink floss for Wrapped Flower. Bring floss up at edge of 4 green gold Cross Stitches. Loosely wrap floss around stitches 3 times. Tack loops down using 1 strand of green gold floss (**Fig. 8**).

Fig. 8

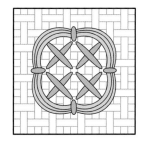

Working Over Two Fabric Threads

Use the sewing method instead of the stab method when working over two fabric threads. Keep your stitching hand on the right side of fabric and take the needle down and up with one stroke. To add support to stitches, it is important that the first Cross Stitch is placed on the fabric with stitch 1–2 beginning and ending where a vertical fabric thread crosses over a horizontal fabric thread (**Fig. 9**). When the first stitch is in the correct position, the entire design will be placed properly, with vertical fabric threads supporting each stitch.

Fig. 9

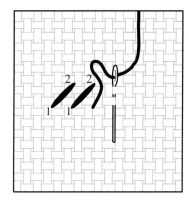

Finding Your Supplies

Fabrics and floss may be found at Cross Stitch shops and limited assortments of items may be found at craft stores. If a shop is not available to you, there are several Cross Stitch shops online. Also, information may be found online at these sites.

Hand-dyed floss: www.thegentleart.com and
　　　www.weeksdyeworks.com
Silk floss: www.needlepointsilk.com
Cotton floss: www.dmc-usa.com and
　　　www.sullivans.net/usa/sullivansfloss/
R&R Reproductions Linens: www.dyeing2stitch.com

Production Team

Writer – Frances Huddleston
Editorial Writer – Susan McManus Johnson
Senior Graphic Artist – Lora Puls
Graphic Artists – Becca Snider and Amy Temple
Photographer – Ken West
Photography Stylist – Sondra Daniel

We have made every effort to ensure that these instructions are accurate and complete. We cannot, however, be responsible for human error, typographical mistakes, or variations in individual work.